Francis Frith's
HEREFORDSHIRE

PHOTOGRAPHIC MEMORIES

Francis Frith's
HEREFORDSHIRE

Dorothy Nicolle

FRITH BOOK Co

First published in the United Kingdom in 2000 by
Frith Book Company Ltd

Hardback Edition 2000
ISBN 1-85937-174-4

Paperback Edition 2002
ISBN 1-85937-567-7

Reprinted in hardback 2002

British Library Cataloguing in Publication Data

Francis Frith's Herefordshire
Dorothy Nicolle

Frith Book Company Ltd
Frith's Barn, Teffont,
Salisbury, Wiltshire SP3 5QP
Tel: +44 (0) 1722 716 376
Email: info@francisfrith.co.uk
www.francisfrith.co.uk

Printed and bound in Great Britain

Front Cover: Hereford, High Town 1891 29285

AS WITH ANY HISTORICAL DATABASE THE FRITH ARCHIVE IS CONSTANTLY BEING CORRECTED AND IMPROVED
AND THE PUBLISHERS WOULD WELCOME INFORMATION ON OMISSIONS OR INACCURACIES

Contents

FRANCIS FRITH: *Victorian Pioneer*

FRANCIS FRITH, Victorian founder of the world-famous photographic archive, was a complex and fascinating man. A devout Quaker and a highly successful Victorian businessman, he was both philosophic by nature and pioneering in outlook.

By 1855 Francis Frith had already established a wholesale grocery business in Liverpool, and sold it for the astonishing sum of £200,000, which is the equivalent today of over £15,000,000. Now a multi-millionaire, he was able to indulge his passion for travel. As a child he had pored over travel books written by early explorers, and his fancy and imagination had been stirred by family holidays to the sublime mountain regions of Wales and Scotland. 'What a land of spirit-stirring and enriching scenes and places!' he had written. He was to return to these scenes of grandeur in later years to 'recapture the thousands of vivid and tender memories', but with a different purpose. Now in his thirties, and captivated by the new science of photography, Frith set out on a series of pioneering journeys to the Nile regions that occupied him from 1856 until 1860.

INTRIGUE AND ADVENTURE

He took with him on his travels a specially-designed wicker carriage that acted as both dark-room and sleeping chamber. These far-flung journeys were packed with intrigue and adventure. In his life story, written when he was sixty-three, Frith tells of being held captive by bandits, and of fighting 'an awful midnight battle to the very point of surrender with a deadly pack of hungry, wild dogs'. Sporting flowing Arab costume, Frith arrived at Akaba by camel seventy years before Lawrence, where he encountered 'desert princes and rival sheikhs, blazing with jewel-hilted swords'.

During these extraordinary adventures he was assiduously exploring the desert regions bordering the Nile and patiently recording the antiquities and peoples with his camera. He was the first photographer to venture beyond the sixth cataract. Africa was still the mysterious 'Dark Continent', and Stanley and Livingstone's historic meeting was a decade into the future. The conditions for picture taking confound belief. He laboured for hours in his wicker dark-room in the sweltering heat of the desert, while the volatile chemicals fizzed dangerously in their trays. Often he was forced to work in remote tombs and caves where conditions

were cooler. Back in London he exhibited his photographs and was 'rapturously cheered' by members of the Royal Society. His reputation as a photographer was made overnight. An eminent modern historian has likened their impact on the population of the time to that on our own generation of the first photographs taken on the surface of the moon.

VENTURE OF A LIFE-TIME

Characteristically, Frith quickly spotted the opportunity to create a new business as a specialist publisher of photographs. He lived in an era of immense and sometimes violent change. For the poor in the early part of Victoria's reign work was a drudge and the hours long, and people had precious little free time to enjoy themselves.

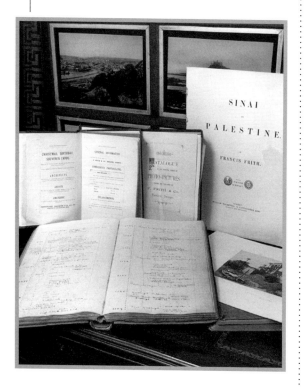

Most had no transport other than a cart or gig at their disposal, and had not travelled far beyond the boundaries of their own town or village. However, by the 1870s, the railways had threaded their way across the country, and Bank Holidays and half-day Saturdays had been made obligatory by Act of Parliament. All of a sudden the ordinary working man and his family were able to enjoy days out and see a little more of the world.

With characteristic business acumen, Francis Frith foresaw that these new tourists would enjoy having souvenirs to commemorate their days out. In 1860 he married Mary Ann Rosling and set out with the intention of photographing every city, town and village in Britain. For the next thirty years he travelled the country by train and by pony and trap, producing fine photographs of seaside resorts and beauty spots that were keenly bought by millions of Victorians. These prints were painstakingly pasted into family albums and pored over during the dark nights of winter, rekindling precious memories of summer excursions.

THE RISE OF FRITH & CO

Frith's studio was soon supplying retail shops all over the country. To meet the demand he gathered about him a small team of photographers, and published the work of independent artist-photographers of the calibre of Roger Fenton and Francis Bedford. In order to gain some understanding of the scale of Frith's business one only has to look at the catalogue issued by Frith & Co in 1886: it

runs to some 670 pages, listing not only many thousands of views of the British Isles but also many photographs of most European countries, and China, Japan, the USA and Canada – note the sample page shown above from the hand-written *Frith & Co* ledgers detailing pictures taken. By 1890 Frith had created the greatest specialist photographic publishing company in the world, with over 2,000 outlets – more than the combined number that Boots and WH Smith have today! The picture on the right shows the *Frith & Co* display board at Ingleton in the Yorkshire Dales. Beautifully constructed with mahogany frame and gilt inserts, it could display up to a dozen local scenes.

POSTCARD BONANZA

The ever-popular holiday postcard we know today took many years to develop. In 1870 the Post Office issued the first plain cards, with a pre-printed stamp on one face. In 1894 they allowed other publishers' cards to be sent through the mail with an attached adhesive halfpenny stamp. Demand grew rapidly, and in 1895 a new size of postcard

was permitted called the court card, but there was little room for illustration. In 1899, a year after Frith's death, a new card measuring 5.5 x 3.5 inches became the standard format, but it was not until 1902 that the divided back came into being, with address and message on one face and a full-size illustration on the other. *Frith & Co* were in the vanguard of postcard development, and Frith's sons Eustace and Cyril continued their father's monumental task, expanding the number of views offered to the public and recording more and more places in Britain, as the coasts and countryside were opened up to mass travel.

Francis Frith died in 1898 at his villa in Cannes, his great project still growing. The archive he created continued in business for another seventy years. By 1970 it contained over a third of a million pictures of 7,000 cities, towns and villages. The massive photographic record Frith has left to us stands as a living monument to a special and very remarkable man.

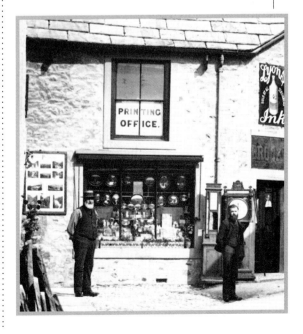

Frith's Archive: *A Unique Legacy*

FRANCIS FRITH'S legacy to us today is of immense significance and value, for the magnificent archive of evocative photographs he created provides a unique record of change in 7,000 cities, towns and villages throughout Britain over a century and more. Frith and his fellow studio photographers revisited locations many times down the years to update their views, compiling for us an enthralling and colourful pageant of British life and character.

We tend to think of Frith's sepia views of Britain as nostalgic, for most of us use them to conjure up memories of places in our own lives with which we have family associations. It often makes us forget that to Francis Frith they were records of daily life as it was actually being lived in the cities, towns and villages of his day. The Victorian age was one of great and often bewildering change for ordinary people, and though the pictures evoke an impression of slower times, life was as busy and hectic as it is today.

We are fortunate that Frith was a photographer of the people, dedicated to recording the minutiae of everyday life. For it is this sheer wealth of visual data, the painstaking chronicle of changes in dress, transport, street layouts, buildings, housing, engineering and landscape that captivates us so much today. His remarkable images offer us a powerful link with the past and with the lives of our ancestors.

TODAY'S TECHNOLOGY

Computers have now made it possible for Frith's many thousands of images to be accessed almost instantly. In the Frith archive today, each photograph is carefully 'digitised' then stored on a CD Rom. Frith archivists can locate a single photograph amongst thousands within seconds. Views can be catalogued and sorted under a variety of categories of place and content to the immediate benefit of researchers. Inexpensive reference prints can be created for them at the touch of a mouse button, and a wide range of books and other printed materials assembled and published for a wider, more general readership - in the next twelve months over a hundred Frith local history titles will be published! The day-to-

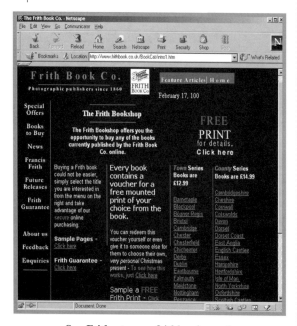

See Frith at www. frithbook.co.uk

day workings of the archive are very different from how they were in Francis Frith's time: imagine the herculean task of sorting through eleven tons of glass negatives as Frith had to do to locate a particular sequence of pictures! Yet the archive still prides itself on maintaining the same high standards of excellence laid down by Francis Frith, including the painstaking cataloguing and indexing of every view.

It is curious to reflect on how the internet now allows researchers in America and elsewhere greater instant access to the archive than Frith himself ever enjoyed. Many thousands of individual views can be called up on screen within seconds on one of the Frith internet sites, enabling people living continents away to revisit the streets of their ancestral home town, or view places in Britain where they have enjoyed holidays. Many overseas researchers welcome the chance to view special theme selections, such as transport, sports, costume and ancient monuments.

We are certain that Francis Frith would have heartily approved of these modern developments, for he himself was always working at the very limits of Victorian photographic technology.

THE VALUE OF THE ARCHIVE TODAY

Because of the benefits brought by the computer, Frith's images are increasingly studied by social historians, by researchers into genealogy and ancestory, by architects, town planners, and by teachers and schoolchildren involved in local history projects. In addition, the archive offers every one of us a unique opportunity to examine the places where we and our families have lived and worked down the years. Immensely successful in Frith's own era, the archive is now, a century and more on, entering a new phase of popularity.

THE PAST IN TUNE WITH THE FUTURE

Historians consider the Francis Frith Collection to be of prime national importance. It is the only archive of its kind remaining in private ownership and has been valued at a million pounds. However, this figure is now rapidly increasing as digital technology enables more and more people around the world to enjoy its benefits.

Francis Frith's archive is now housed in an historic timber barn in the beautiful village of Teffont in Wiltshire. Its founder would not recognize the archive office as it is today. In place of the many thousands of dusty boxes containing glass plate negatives and an all-pervading odour of photographic chemicals, there are now ranks of computer screens. He would be amazed to watch his images travelling round the world at unimaginable speeds through network and internet lines.

The archive's future is both bright and exciting. Francis Frith, with his unshakeable belief in making photographs available to the greatest number of people, would undoubtedly approve of what is being done today with his lifetime's work. His photographs, depicting our shared past, are now bringing pleasure and enlightenment to millions around the world a century and more after his death.

HEREFORDSHIRE - *An Introduction*

Of all the counties England can record,
Few are so blessed as this of Hereford
For wheat and wool, and wood and water famed,
And for good cider very much esteemed.
Few counties can afford a better place
For fishing, fowling, or the healthy chase:
England has not more rich or fertile fields,
None that a better annual produce yields. ...

Thomas Parker, a joiner living in Kington in the north-west of the county, wrote those lines in around 1785. More than two hundred years later, all that he said remains true. Herefordshire is a beautiful county, almost unknown to many people who live elsewhere.

Talk to people in other parts of Britain about the county and you can get quite blank expressions, and remarks like - it's somewhere in the west, isn't it? Somewhere near Wales, or is it in Wales? Yes, I know Herefordshire - cider and cattle. For many people, that about sums up their knowledge; perhaps it is for this reason that the county retains so much of its charm today, a charm that can be seen so clearly in the photographs taken by Francis Frith.

It is a county where two cultures - the Celtic west and the Anglo-Saxon east - met and mingled. But it goes back further than that. Two thousand years ago Britain was occupied by a variety of Celtic tribes living side by side. Sometimes they were at peace with each other. More often, judging by their numerous hill forts, they were at war. This intertribal warfare in Britain came to an

end with the arrival of the Romans. They settled in the lowland areas, but they also wanted control over those Britons who continued to live in the hills; the region that is now Herefordshire was used as a springboard for the Roman legions to control those living in the hills. So even then, the region was already a border - between rural, settled lowland and wild upland.

With the departure of the Romans in the 5th century, we enter a period in Britain known to us now as the Dark Ages. Little is known about the people who lived then. Many Roman sites were abandoned. Some people had recently become Christians. Did the newly Christianised Britons manage to hold onto their new faith? It is quite probable that they did, since we know of quite a few ancient Celtic saints in Herefordshire of around that period whose names survive in some of the early churches - names like Dyfrig and Dewi. However, with little or no contact with Christians elsewhere, it must have been hard for local people to cling on to their religion. In fact, with the flood of new, pagan settlers arriving from the east, it is a wonder that the names of these saints survive today.

These new settlers were the Angles and Saxons, who ultimately were to give us the language we speak today, and even the name of our country - Angleland or England. We can see, just from looking at a map, where these people settled from the English names they gave to their settlements. Yet in Herefordshire the picture becomes confused. It was here that Anglo-Saxons met Britons (or Welsh, as they came to call them). Sometimes Welsh names are to be found in the east of the county, such as the village of Llangarron in the south-east, which is surrounded by settlements whose names begin with Pen and Tre. But you can travel westwards and find English names such as Kington, Madley and Peterchurch. And then there are those wonderful names that mix the two languages - is Dilwyn English or Welsh? And Leominster, for example - the name means English minster church in Leon, the Anglicised version of an old Celtic name.

It was at this time that the whole region became known as the Marches, meaning borders. This was border country. It separated the English from the Welsh - evidence of this demarcation is to be found in the line of Offa's Dyke, which was built by the great king of Mercia. It is surprising that as it goes along the western border of Herefordshire the dyke does not seem to be the great earthwork that it is further north - does this imply that here, at least, relations across the border were reasonably good at the time? Perhaps this would explain that total mix of English and Welsh placenames we have locally.

That is not to say that life was always peaceful here. Armies have always passed through

Herefordshire. Even the name of the county's capital reminds us of that: the name means 'the ford where the army crossed' (the word 'here' is a Saxon word for an army). We must assume it was an English army, since the word is English, but whose was it, and when did it cross the ford and first settle there? By the 11th century there was a permanent fortification by the town guarding the ford and controlling whosoever should pass by. Not that it was always effective - the city was burnt down by the Welsh in 1055, and Edward the Confessor sent an army to rout them.

For years the border was an area of constant strife, but as the centuries passed the warfare took on more of the nature of civil wars. The 15th century saw the Wars of the Roses, as the royal houses of York and Lancaster battled for control of the throne. One battle took place in the north of the county at Mortimer's Cross. Two centuries later, Hereford itself was to be affected by another civil war when as a Royalist centre it was taken (more than once) by Parliamentarian forces. Incidentally, the military tradition still continues in Herefordshire: today the county is the home base for the SAS.

However, it has always been more peaceful pursuits that have been important in the county. When people think today of Herefordshire they think of a rural heritage - Herefordshire cattle and Herefordshire cider. Hereford cattle are predominantly red in colour, but can always be distinguished by their white faces. As a breed they were probably originally a cross between an ancient breed of white Welsh cattle crossed with a smaller, possibly Roman, breed of red cattle. Thus they go back a long way, but as a breed they were not developed until the 1700s. Today, if ever you watch a cowboy film you will see that many of the cattle have white faces; they have been bred with Herefords, which are particularly hardy and can cope with the extremes of climate in the western states of America, and in many other parts of the world too. But in the county itself ... well, these days you can wander for hours looking for Herefords amongst the foreign imported breeds that predominate here now.

But it is still easy to see signs of the county's other rural tradition - apple orchards for cider. There are ten thousand acres of apple orchards here today, growing around twenty different varieties of apple which will be mixed together to produce the cider. Cider was probably first produced here over two thousand years ago by the Celts, who are known to have worshipped an Apple God. Today it is big business; Bulmers, the main local cider producer, has on its site the largest alcohol container in the world - a tank that can hold over one and a half million gallons of liquid.

Is it any wonder that cider has played an

important part in local tradition and writings? There is even a Bible named for it: when Wycliffe translated the Bible into English in around 1420, his assistant, Nicholas of Hereford, translated the words 'strong drink' in St John's Gospel as 'cider'. To this day this version of the Bible is known as the Cider Bible, and a copy can be seen at the world-famous chained library at Hereford's cathedral, a reminder of the importance that cathedrals played in the past as centres of learning and the arts.

And why is it that so many of the famous people this county has produced have achieved their fame in the arts, particularly poetry, music and acting? Is it something to do with the local air, perhaps? Herefordshire claims to be the birthplace of William Langland, writer of the poem 'Piers Plowman' in the 1300s. Mind you, Shropshire claims him too. Poets abound - Elizabeth Barrett Browning and John Masefield are both associated with Ledbury. Ledbury was also associated with the Dymock poets (Rupert Brooke, the American Robert Frost, and others) in the years before the First World War. The little village of Dymock is actually just across the border in Gloucestershire, but Ledbury was their nearest town. Today the town still attracts poets and people interested in poetry to an annual ten-day-long poetry festival held each summer.

So many of our favourite stories must have been first told centuries ago. Today such tales are fast disappearing. Fortunately, in the early years of the 20th century many of the old Herefordshire stories and legends were collected and published by Ella Mary Leather. Mrs Leather used to travel around the county, meeting gypsies and farm labourers, in order to collect tales directly from the storytellers. She also worked with Ralph Vaughan Williams, the composer, who similarly collected songs and music before they died out and were forgotten.

But when we speak of music in Herefordshire, we speak of just one man: Edward Elgar. He was born just over the county boundary in Worcestershire, but was very deeply influenced by Herefordshire. Actually, the county's connection with music goes back way before Edward Elgar to the 1700s, when the three choirs of the three local cathedral cities (Hereford, Worcester and Gloucester) decided to hold a 'musick meeting'. It is said to be the oldest music festival in Europe (as opposed to festivals for other purposes where music is played) and it is hosted by the three cities in turn. The early meetings lasted for two days, and the music was a mixture of religious music played in the cathedral and of secular music, which would be played in the evenings at other venues. Today we would consider Handel's 'Messiah' to be sacred in style, but it was not always so: it was 1759, the year of Handel's death,

before the piece was first performed in an English cathedral - in Hereford. Elgar's association with the festival began in 1878 when he played with the second violins. Later he lived in Hereford, and he was living here when he composed some of his greatest work; just a few months before his death, he ended his career by conducting at the Hereford festival.

The acting profession is also well represented - Nell Gwynne came from Hereford. Again, other places claim her, but I think Hereford's claim is probably better than most. Today she is far better known for something other than acting. Someone who will always be associated with nothing but acting is an 18th-century actor whose name is used for theatres all over the world to this day: David Garrick was born in the city in 1717.

The county of Herefordshire has been around for many centuries. We can only guess when the settlement that gave the county its name was first founded - probably before the mid 7th century, when the cathedral was founded. It was a further two hundred years before England was divided into administrative areas known as shires and the shire of Herefordshire was established. The county continued in existence for over one thousand years. Then in the 1970s the powers that be decided it could not work, and that it should be joined with the neighbouring county of Worcestershire. Neither county wanted the union. It could best be described as a shot-gun wedding with both parties being forced to the altar. People said it would never work, and so it turned out. Thirty years later, an amicable divorce was arranged: Herefordshire is now a county in its own right once again. Long may it remain so.

Bromyard, Broad Street c1906 B229301

In and Around Hereford

HEREFORD, THE RIVER WYE 1925 77333

HEREFORD
The River Wye 1925
The name Hereford means 'the ford for the army'. Which army it was that gave the place its name we cannot begin to guess at, but for a settlement close to the English-Welsh border that has seen numerous armies pass by, the name is very appropriate.

HEREFORD
The Cathedral and Bridge 1890
Anyone standing here today would be mown down by traffic crossing over the new bridge. The cathedral was founded in 676AD; nearly 150 years later it became an important site of pilgrimage with the establishment of a shrine to St Ethelbert, who was murdered (probably by King Offa) in 794AD.

HEREFORD, THE CATHEDRAL AND BRIDGE 1890 26957

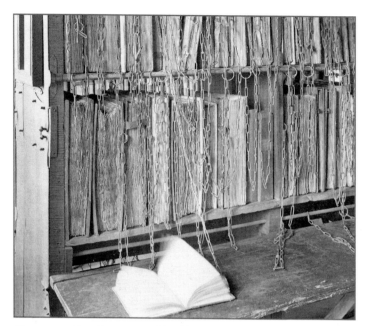

HEREFORD, THE CATHEDRAL, THE CHAINED LIBRARY 1925 77352

HEREFORD, THE CATHEDRAL
The Chained Library 1925
This is the largest chained library in the world, with some 1,500 books and manuscripts some dating from the 8th century. The best-known manuscript is the Mappa Mundi, one of the four oldest maps in the world. The entire collection was recently rehoused (using the old shelves pictured here) in a new purpose-built library.

HEREFORD
Broad Street 1891
It is difficult today to imagine Broad Street with so little traffic. The fabulously ornate building on the left is the City Library, Museum and Art Gallery, which was opened in 1874. Notice how the carriages are apparently 'parked' and waiting in the middle of the street.

HEREFORD, BROAD STREET 1891 29284

HEREFORD, BROAD STREET 1925 77341

All Saints Church, at the top of the street, is still a church holding regular services. Yet the interior has been restyled in a very modern way to house a coffee shop and other facilities. For some people, the styling may be too modern. Personally, I love it, and I wish more churches could follow suit.

HEREFORD, CASTLE GREEN BOWLS 1910 62503

This is the site of Hereford Castle. The first castle was built around 1048 and was destroyed by the Welsh in 1055 - before the Norman Conquest. The column commemorates Lord Nelson, who was a frequent visitor to Hereford and a Freeman of the City. The column was built in 1806-09 after he died at Trafalgar.

HEREFORD, HIGH TOWN 1891 29286
High Town is still the main shopping area in Hereford. It was once known as the Butchery, where meat was sold; the arms of the Butcher's Guild can be seen over the front door on the other side of the building in the foreground. Notice the decorator up on his ladder in the distance.

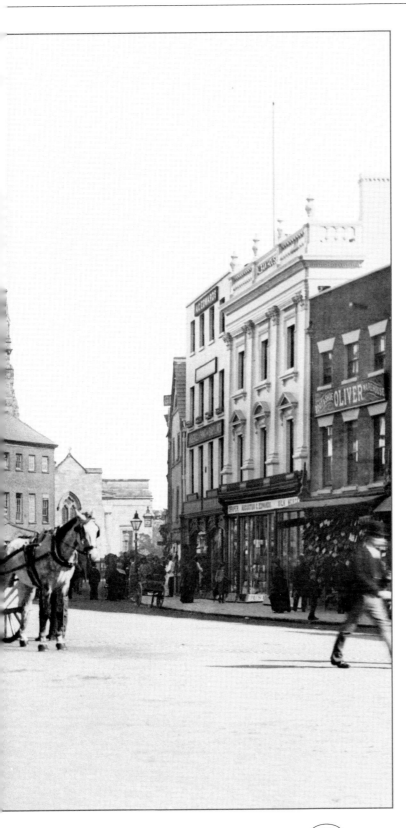

HEREFORD, HIGH TOWN 1891 29285
Today the Old House, as the timber-framed building is known, is a museum. The house was built in 1621; inside there are lovely examples of period furniture, including a delightful 17th-century baby-walker!

HEREFORD, HIGH TOWN 1898 41751

That ladder that we saw page 20 is still there - surely they have finished decorating by now! Notice the bus disappearing down the road with its steps up to the top deck. Today High Town is a pedestrian area, with trees planted in the middle of the road and plenty of places to sit.

HEREFORD, HIGH TOWN 1925 77336

Nell Gwynne, orange seller, actress and mistress to Charles II, is believed to have been born in Hereford. Other places make the same claim, but the diarist Samuel Pepys mentioned a conversation with Nell in his diary in which she spoke of her early life in Hereford. He described her as 'pretty, witty Nell'.

HEREFORD, COMMERCIAL STREET 1891 29288

This street has totally changed. But notice the copper kettle hanging on the left - it is still there. Once an ironmongers, and now a bookshop, the building may be totally different, but it is one of the terms of the lease that the kettle (with a smaller kettle attached to its spout) should continue to hang there.

HEREFORD, THE CONINGSBY HOSPITAL c1955 H74010

Now a museum, the Coningsby Hospital was built in 1614 as a retirement home for old soldiers. The men housed here were provided with red uniforms: it is thought that Nell Gwynne persuaded Charles II to found the Chelsea Pensioners Hospital in London and to model it on this Hereford version.

MUCH BIRCH
The Church c1960
The placename means the big (or larger) place with the birch tree - as opposed to Little Birch nearby, which presumably also had a birch tree!

MUCH BIRCH
The Axe and Cleaver Hotel c1960
The name of this pub, which still sits by the A49, reminds us of the local importance of the meat trade and butchers. In fact, the locality is called The Cleaver - did it take its name from an early pub of that name?

MUCH BIRCH, THE CHURCH C1960 M182001

MUCH BIRCH, THE AXE AND CLEAVER HOTEL C1960 M182003

PETERSTOW, THE POST OFFICE AND THE VILLAGE STORES c1960 P173001

PETERSTOW
The Post Office and the Village Stores c1960
The sign reads 'STOP! for teas neath the apple trees'. It is a reminder of the importance of apples (and therefore cider) in the local economy. In the 18th century part of a labourer's wage was paid in cider and a farmer with a reputation for good cider would always get the best workers.

PETERSTOW
The Yewtree Inn c1960
We are continuing with the drinks theme: today this pub has the most delightful pub sign - a picture of a topiary mug. Cider was locally seen as a cure for a range of ailments such as gout, and was also used for cleansing wounds.

PETERSTOW, THE YEWTREE INN c1960 P173004

BRAMPTON ABBOTTS, THE CHURCH c1960 B424501

In medieval times babies were sometimes baptised in cider - until the church actually banned the practice. Perhaps it happened here. The village of Brampton Abbotts was also home, during World War Two, to Chelsea Pensioners who were evacuated here.

Downstream Along The Wye Valley

ROSS-ON-WYE
From the River 1893 32423
There is a story that Ross was once called Rose-town because
it 'rose gradually up the hill from the river'. In fact, it comes
from Welsh 'rhos' meaning hill or promontory. When viewed
from across the River Wye, the Royal Hotel still dominates the
skyline as it has done since it opened in 1837.

ROSS-ON-WYE, THE OLD CASTLE c1960 R57031
The castle is not actually in Ross, but is just over the river in the village of Bridstow, where it guards the river crossing. This river crossing was vitally important; as a result, there has been a settlement by the river here since Roman times.

ROSS-ON-WYE, THE RIVER WYE 1901 47887
Rowing is a popular activity all along the River Wye, and in Ross there is now a Rowing Club on the banks of the river just to the left of this picture.

ROSS-ON-WYE, THE RIVER WYE 1901 47887A

Notice the man on the right carrying his coracle on his back. Coracles, made of leather stretched over a wooden frame, date from ancient times. Indeed, it is thought the name comes from the Latin word 'corium' meaning animal hide. They are very difficult to manoeuvre, but are silent in the water - ideal for poachers!

ROSS-ON-WYE, THE HOPE AND ANCHOR HOTEL c1955 R57006

The town grew beside a fording point across the river. Later there was a ferry crossing here. In a tragic accident the ferry overturned and over thirty people drowned, so that a stone bridge (that survives to this day) was built nearby in 1599.

ROSS-ON-WYE, THE TOWER C1965 R57105
It looks magnificent on the skyline, and visitors immediately assume that it is a survival of the medieval town walls.
Not a bit. The tower is a total fake built in 1833 when the road beside it was being constructed.

ROSS-ON-WYE, THE MARKET HOUSE c1878 10571
This is a very early but particularly pleasing photograph in the Francis Frith collection. The Market House was built around 1650, and the cupola was probably added some fifty years later when the first clock was installed. It is now used as a Heritage Centre for the town.

ROSS-ON-WYE, THE MARKET HOUSE 1893 32427
The roundel in the building contains a bust of Charles II. It was put there by John Kyrle, who is better known as the Man of Ross. He was a philanthropist who did an amazing amount of good for the town - introducing a decent water supply, donating a library, restoring the church spire - the list is endless.

ROSS-ON-WYE
THE MARKET HOUSE 1914 67700
The three boys are standing below a billboard which reads 'Special Grave Emergency 100,000 men wanted at once'. It is part of the recruitment drive for the Great War. Note, also, the wonderful car on the left.

ROSS-ON-WYE, MARKET DAY c1960 R57064

John Kyrle's house is the timber building behind the Market. He died in 1724, and the entire population of the town attended his funeral - he was described as 'a genuine Herefordshire man with a spade on his shoulder and a glass bottle of liquor (always beer or cider) in his hand'.

ROSS-ON-WYE, HIGH STREET 1906 54484

John Kyrle may have liked a drink, but not everyone approved. On the right of this picture is the sign of the Wye Valley Temperance Hotel - the temperance movement was a direct result of too much drunkenness amongst the working classes in the 1800s. Another advertisement peeps out above the awning:- 'accommodation for cyclists'.

WESTON UNDER PENYARD, THE POST OFFICE c1965 W308029

The building housing the post office and shop is now totally rendered, and is a private house called The Olde Shoppe. The telephone kiosk still survives, however. Everyone has heard of the nursery rhyme 'Oranges and Lemons'. The Herefordshire version says of the local church 'Stick a goose and dress un, say the bells of Wesson'.

WESTON UNDER PENYARD, THE WESTON CROSS INN c1965 W308004

The Weston Cross Inn is still easily recognisable except for two things. Firstly, the ivy has grown considerably in the last 45 years. Secondly, the modern road goes through the building to the left - it has been cut off just behind the old pub sign. Unfortunately, the pretty little iron road sign has also disappeared.

WESTON UNDER PENYARD, THE VICARAGE c1955 W308011

ROSS-ON-WYE, THE CHASE c1955 R57060

WESTON UNDER PENYARD
The Vicarage c1955

It is amazing how a building can change. This is now the Hunsdon Manor Hotel: there is a new porch, the three windows have been heightened, and a conservatory has been added to the right. Even little crenellations have been built onto the old three-sided extension. In fact, it is almost totally unrecognisable.

ROSS-ON-WYE
The Chase c1955

The word 'chase' in a place-name in medieval times indicated an area set aside exclusively for hunting. These areas were not necessarily forested in the past, although today much of this area is covered in woodland.

GOODRICH CASTLE 1893

Goodrich Castle was one of a series of important castles guarding the English-Welsh border. It was once owned by the Clare family, who are said to have brought soil over from Ireland to form the beaten earth floors so that 'no toad could live in it', a reminder of the general living conditions at the time.

◆

GOODRICH CASTLE
Kerne Bridge c1960

The River Wye at this point is said to be haunted by the ghosts of Alice Birch and Charles Gifford. Fleeing from nearby Goodrich Castle during the Civil War, they drowned while trying to cross the river; whenever there is a storm, their cries can still be heard.

GOODRICH CASTLE 1893 32453

GOODRICH CASTLE, KERNE BRIDGE c1960 G31001

THE WYE VALLEY, WELSH BICKNOR 1893 32446

SYMONDS YAT, VIEW FROM YAT ROCK 1914 67662

THE WYE VALLEY
Welsh Bicknor 1893
Despite its name, Welsh Bicknor, like English
Bicknor across the river, is in England. This
settlement, however, is on the west (or Welsh) side
of the river. Further downstream the River Wye does
indeed become the English-Welsh border.

◆

SYMONDS YAT
View from Yat Rock 1914
The view from Yat Rock is superb: it must be one of
the best viewpoints in England. The railway line in
the photograph is now disused, and parts of the line
are used as trails through the forest.

THE WYE VALLEY, HORSESHOE BEND 1893 32490

Notice the boats on the river in the foreground. It is difficult to tell whether they are pleasure boats or working ones. It was in 1745 that the Reverend John Egerton first arranged boat trips for friends down the river from Ross, and so began a thriving tourist trade that continues to this day.

SYMONDS YAT, THE RIVER WYE AND DOWARD HILL 1914 67650

This is another view from Yat Rock. The word 'yat' means a gate or gap. Symond was Robert Symond, High Sheriff for the county in the 1600s; by controlling the gate here, he would have controlled all river trade in and out of Herefordshire.

SYMONDS YAT
THE RAILWAY STATION 1898 42742
One of the billboards refers to the Great Western (often better known as God's Wonderful) Railway. The billboard on the right indicates an amalgamation - the GW and Mid(lands) Railway Co, Severn and Wye Joint Railway. Photographers were obviously unusual at the time - everyone on the platform is watching the Frith photographer very carefully.

SYMONDS YAT, THE RAILWAY STATION 1893 32436
By Victorian times the area all along this stretch of the River Wye was becoming popular with tourists from all over the country, and this was owing to the accessibility provided by the railways.

SYMONDS YAT, THE ROYAL HOTEL 1898 42738
The station is the small building on the right, now demolished to make way for a carpark. A brochure (undated, unfortunately) advertises rates at the hotel as ranging from £4 4/- to £5 5/- per person per week. There were additional charges - for example, a cold bath would cost 6d or a hot bath 1/-!

Symonds Yat, The Royal Hotel 1898 42740

The same brochure asks potential customers to 'please note the name - and address - and so avoid confusion with another Hotel which is three-quarters of a mile distant - on the other side of the river'. Obviously competition between the two was very strong.

Symonds Yat, The Wye Rapids Hotel from the Rock c1955 S247064

This is the rival hotel referred to above; judging by the painted stones in its garden, it is doing its best to advertise itself to anyone visiting the Symonds Yat viewpoint. Today, the Wye Rapids Hotel is just a memory, even the building has disappeared, while the Royal is still going strong.

SYMONDS YAT, THE FERRY 1914 67659
This ferry ran between the two hotels. Of dozens that used to exist between Ross and Chepstow, only two (including this one) survive. It is a rope ferry; in this photograph we can see the ferryman pulling on the rope to take his passengers across the river. Today it costs 60p to cross the river.

THE WYE VALLEY, NEW WEIR FROM THE FERRY C1878 10561

This is another very early photograph in the Frith collection. It strikes me as being a beautiful and carefully-posed picture, with the lady in the foreground reading her book. She may be enjoying being outside, but notice how she is totally protected from the sunshine.

SYMONDS YAT, THE RIVER 1893 32444

These boats are obviously waiting for human passengers. In times past, when goods were being taken up and down river, the boats were hauled upriver by horses using towpaths. Sometimes the horses would need to cross the river, and originally many of the ferry crossings were for these horses.

SYMONDS YAT, DOWARD HILL 1893 32441

With the introduction of reliable roads, and then a railway system, this area would have economically died had it not been for the arrival of tourists. Transporting goods by river was a slow business - for example, the road from here to Hereford is only 14 miles long, while the river route is 48 miles.

WHITCHURCH, THE VILLAGE c1955 W582003

The building on the right is the Crown Hotel; the sign tells us that it is 'the first hotel in England'. A dual carriageway now runs straight through it, but the Crown still exists - it now occupies the building across the road.

THE WYE VALLEY, SEVEN SISTERS ROCK 1914 67664
The views all along this stretch of the Wye are spectacular at every turn. To see the best view here involves a dizzily steep climb. It is one of the more remote, or less accessible, viewpoints locally, and this has probably helped with the recent successful reintroduction of peregrine falcons in the area.

The Golden Valley and The South-West

MUCH DEWCHURCH
The Memorial c1960 M183003
Dewchurch means the church of Dewi, who was probably a
local Celtic saint. However, since the name Dewi is Welsh for
David, in later centuries it was thought that the village had a
connection with St David, Wales's patron saint. We are quite
close to the Welsh border here, after all.

◆

MUCH DEWCHURCH, THE BLACK SWAN c1960 M183001
Timbers in the Black Swan were found to date to the 14th century while work was recently being done to renovate the building.

ORCOP HILL, THE POST OFFICE c1955 O62002
It is difficult to recognise this building today. For example, the front door has been blocked up and the main entrance is now at the rear, away from the roadside.

ORCOP HILL, THE FOUNTAIN INN c1955 O62009

ORCOP HILL
The Fountain Inn c1955

'Orcop, God help us' is a local saying - I wonder why. Once there were five pubs in the parish of Orcop; today this is the only one that survives. Renowned locally for its restaurant, specialising in fish dishes, it draws people from a wide area.

ABBEY DORE
The Church 1898

This is an enormous church for such a small village. Yet it is far smaller than it was - today's church consists only of the chancel and transept from the original building. It was a Cistercian abbey; since the Cistercians always lived in very remote regions, it is unusual to find such a building surviving at all.

ABBEY DORE, THE CHURCH 1898 41759

EWYAS HAROLD, THE VILLAGE C1965 E181012

This strange placename is pronounced U-iss Harold. It obviously once belonged (in the 11th century) to a man named Harold, but there is argument as to what exactly Ewyas means. Some references say sheep town, some say deer town - certainly both creatures would have been common locally.

EWYAS HAROLD, DULAS ROAD C1965 E181014

Following the Norman conquest, Ewyas Harold was given by William I to William FitzOsbern, who was made Earl of Hereford. FitzOsbern had certainly earned his new lands and title - he gave the Conqueror sixty ships for the invasion of 1066.

Ewyas Harold, The Village from the Common c1960 E181004
Notice the sturdy tower of St Michael's church. We are close to the border here, and this tower, with its seven-foot-thick walls, would have been an important lookout point when it was built in the 1200s. At that time it was free-standing.

Ewyas Harold, Dulas Court c1960 E181018
Sitting by the Dulas Brook, this house has a lovely setting. Things were not always so calm - legend has it that there was once a fierce battle near here with the Welsh fighting against Edward I. So many died that the brook ran red with their blood for three days after the battle.

EWYAS HAROLD
The Common c1960

Local people have the right, although I doubt whether it is used much these days, to take water from nearby St Martin's Well. Its waters reputedly have healing powers for those people with eye complaints.

CLODOCK
The Village and the Church c1960

Prince Clydowg was murdered near here. His body was placed on a cart to be taken for burial, but when the oxen reached the River Monnow they refused to cross. Nothing would make them move, and so it was decided to build a church right here in which to bury the prince, who promptly became venerated as a saint.

EWYAS HAROLD, THE COMMON c1960 E181003

CLODOCK, THE VILLAGE AND THE CHURCH c1960 C332002

CLODOCK
The Mill c1960
The enormous water wheel , visible on the left, was made in Leominster in 1868. Today, the mill is no longer working as a mill.

WHITNEY
The Bridge c1955
The toll bridge was built in 1802. One toll-keeper was a witch; when a farmer refused to pay, she stopped his animals 'with a single look' so that they could not move until the farmer paid up! Today you are on trust to drop your 50p in the box as you drive past.

CLODOCK, THE MILL c1960 C332001

WHITNEY, THE BRIDGE c1955 W307008

WHITNEY, THE CHURCH AND THE WYE VALLEY c1955 W307007
This scene has hardly changed today, although the road gets busier with each passing year. A local man, Allan Lewis, won the Victoria Cross in September 1918 at Ronsoy in France.

Kington and The Black & White Trail

EARDISLEY
THE VILLAGE c1950 E106002
Nikolaus Pevsner in his book on the county says of Eardisley: 'the village has a proper street, which is not all that frequent in Herefordshire'. In fact, Eardisley is still very much a village that grew along a street.

EARDISLEY, THE TRAM INN C1950 E106003

Today the Tram Inn has a picture on its sign depicting the old tram. It was a horse-drawn tramway, opened in 1820, and was used to bring tubs of coal from Brecon. It was replaced in 1864 by a proper railway but that, too, closed in the 1960s.

EARDISLEY, THE VILLAGE C1955 E106027

Sir Conan Doyle based his story 'The Hound of the Baskervilles' on a legend about a hound from Hell at nearby Kington. The Baskerville family came to England with William the Conqueror, and were lords of the manor of Eardisley for many hundreds of years.

KINGTON, BRIDGE STREET c1955 K98049

In 1055 the Welsh came across the border and ravaged Hereford, burning the cathedral there. In retaliation, forces were sent into Wales by Edward the Confessor. As a result, this area came under the control of the King; hence its name - King's town.

KINGTON, HIGH STREET c1955 K98047

On the right of the street you can just make out the sign for the Ewe and Lamb Inn. The town had a distinct advantage in being right on the Welsh border: on Sundays, when the pubs were all closed in Wales, a thirsty Welshman could always find a drink just over the border in Kington.

KINGTON, THE CROSS c1955 K98030

'This town was awake only once a week ... on market day. If you had passed through it at any other time you may have seen the shops open and the houses open, and a few persons walking about the streets with their eyes open; but the shops and the houses and the people therein were all asleep'. So wrote a local historian in 1845.

KINGTON, OLD MARKET HALL c1965 K98076

The Market Hall was built in 1885, although the tower was added some years later. Notice the signpost in front of the building - it is actually an old cast-iron water pump.

KINGTON, VIEW FROM THE CHURCH C1965 K98064

Inside the church is the tomb of Ellen the Terrible. When her brother was murdered, she sought vengeance by disguising herself as a man and entering an archery contest; when it was her turn to shoot, she fired her arrow at point-blank range at the murderer. In the confusion that followed she escaped.

TITLEY, THE CHURCH C1960 T162001

This is the fifth church on this site. One of the previous churches fell into disrepair at the time of the Black Death, another was burnt down by Owen Glendower. A grave in the churchyard is that of Lazar Meszaros, a Hungarian freedom fighter who died while on a visit here in 1858.

LYONSHALL, THE VILLAGE c1965 L218001

We are close to the English-Welsh border here, with Offa's Dyke less than a mile away. Even the place's name is partly Celtic: Lyon (or Leon) was the Anglo-Saxon name for this region, but it derives from an Old Welsh word, 'lleoni', meaning easily-flooded. It is from this that a local river, the Lene, gets its name.

LYONSHALL, THE VILLAGE c1965 L218002

The heart of the present village is actually about half a mile away from its original site, where the church and ruined castle still survive. Depopulation following the Black Death in the 14th century led to the abandonment of the old village site.

SARNESFIELD, SARNESFIELD COURT HOTEL c1960 S769025

The hotel pictured here has once again become a private building. The name Sarnesfield is yet another reminder of the local mix of Welsh and Anglo-Saxon. 'Sarn' is a Welsh word meaning road, 'felde' is Anglo-Saxon open land - hence we have the road through open land.

SARNESFIELD, THE CHURCH c1960 S769037

In St Mary's church is the tomb of John Abel, the King's Carpenter, who died in 1674 aged 97. He was given the title when, during the Civil War, he made hand-operated corn mills for the Royalists at Hereford when that city was under siege.

WEOBLEY
THE RED LION c1955 W304069
The Red Lion dates from the 14th century; it has a lovely model of a lion on the corner of the building, which can be seen here. Fortunately it still survives, as does the solitary petrol pump across the road.

WEOBLEY, THE TUDOR TEA ROOM, BROAD STREET c1955 W304110

Weobley, pronounced Webbley, is one of the delightful villages on Herefordshire's aptly named black and white trail. One of the few stone buildings is the church of St Peter and St Paul, of which it has been said: 'Poor Weobley, proud people, low church, high steeple'. Make of that what you will.

WEOBLEY, THE OLDE UNICORN INN c1955 W304004

With the addition of hanging baskets, this street is prettier than ever. Here the buildings are genuine timber-framed buildings. Elsewhere in the village one or two brick houses have been painted black and white; it has been said of the village that 'many girls look all the better for a little added paint work'!

WEOBLEY, KINGTON ROAD C1955 W304002

The village was once a pocket borough returning two members to Parliament. The qualification to vote was that a man should have cooked and eaten a meal here. So voters arrived the night before an election, made fires in the street and cooked a meal over it. They were known as pot-wallopers, a term that soon became an insult.

WEOBLEY, THE LEY C1960 W304132

This beautiful house is thought by many to be the prettiest timber-framed house in the county. It was built in 1589, and the oak timbers have never been painted for a black and white effect, which was often a Victorian idea. Here the timbers have been allowed to weather naturally.

DILWYN, THE VILLAGE c1960 D123003

DILWYN, ST MARY'S CHURCH c1960 D123006

DILWYN
The Village c1960
Dilwyn means the settlement at the secret or shady place - what a delightful name. Some people suggest that the name is simply a Welsh personal name, but I prefer the first meaning.

DILWYN
St Mary's Church c1960
The composer Ralph Vaughan Williams stayed here for a time collecting local folksongs. He worked with Ella Mary Leather who, in 1912, published a book on the county's folklore; it has been described as 'one of the most important works of its kind'. She researched her material amongst local gypsies, farm-labourers and hop-pickers.

PEMBRIDGE, THE PARISH CHURCH C1965 P172025

Notice how the belfry is separate from the church. Work began on it in 1320, but because of the Black Death, it took forty years to complete. Tradition has it that the leather on the door of the church is the skin of a marauding Viking, captured on a raid in the area and skinned alive.

PEMBRIDGE, MARKET PLACE AND THE NEW INN C1955 P172010

Like so many New Inns, this one is actually very old, dating from the 1600s. The delightful market is even older. It is difficult to imagine it as a two-storey structure, which it was originally. Beside it are two stones called nails where deals were agreed or struck.

PEMBRIDGE, THE VILLAGE c1965 P172022
The Greyhound pub has gone, but refreshments can still be obtained here - the building is now a tea shop. The building opposite has been restored and proudly proclaims that the work was carried out in MCMLXXVI - counting in Latin can get rather involved. I make that 1976.

EARDISLAND, THE VILLAGE c1955 E105022
Described by Nikolaus Pevsner as 'an uncommonly pretty village', Eardisland recently won yet another award as the most beautiful village in the Midlands. Today you will find time has again gone back to the 1950s - a lovely old AA phone box has recently been restored and positioned just behind the wall by the market cross.

EARDISLAND, THE VILLAGE 1906 55484

The tall building on the right is an 18th-century dovecote which has only just been restored. Doves (and pigeons) were a vitally important source of food in medieval times. Only the lord of a manor could have a dovecote. Pity the poor tenant farmer who could only watch as his lord's doves ate his corn.

EARDISLAND, THE RIVER ARROW C1960 E105027

Any time there is heavy rain the River Arrow can be guaranteed to flood over its banks. Water frequently rises to cover the garden on the left. The medieval pronunciation of this village was Erleslen, and it is thought that the last part comes from a Welsh word 'llion', meaning floods.

EARDISLAND, THE RIVER ARROW 1906 55486

In 1485, when on his way to fight Richard III at Bosworth Field, Henry Tudor crossed the River Arrow. He recalled a prophecy that 'who should shoot the arrow first' would win the battle. When his men crossed the river they saw this as a good omen, and, of course, went on to win the battle.

EARDISLAND, THE BRIDGE c1955 E105018

The timber building just beyond the bridge is called Bridge Cottage, but is known locally as the Whipping Post House because of an old whipping post that is just below the window in the gable end. The building was once a grammar school - was the post used to keep unruly schoolboys in order?

EARDISLAND, STAICK HOUSE C1960 E105051
Staick House was once the rectory in the village. The word staik probably comes from stank, an old term for a dam across a river. Incidentally, the topiary bush is still there.

Leominster and The North

MONKLAND
All Saints Church 1906 55488
When this photograph was taken, the church had been
thoroughly rebuilt only forty years before, so it is a surprise to
see so much ivy growing up the tower. A former vicar, Sir
Henry Baker, wrote many hymns and was a major compiler of
'Hymns Ancient and Modern'.

MONKLAND, THE RED LION INN 1906 55487

The man standing is a postman in his uniform. Yet the other people would appear to be customers at the pub, which makes one wonder how late in the day the postman was making his visit. Perhaps he was on his second (or even third) delivery round of the day. So much for progress.

HOPE UNDER DINMORE, THE VILLAGE c1955 H264009

Hope is an old word for valley, so we have the village in the valley under the great hill (Welsh 'din mawr'): these old names often make good sense if one can only understand them. Today the area is very popular because the hillside has been planted out as an arboretum, with specimen trees from all over the world.

HOPE UNDER DINMORE, HAMPTON COURT c1955 H264012

The first great house on this site was built by Sir Rowland Lenthall in 1434, using the hostage money he obtained from all the prisoners he took at the Battle of Agincourt! The house we see today, however, was the home of the Arkwright family, the famous cotton-spinning family, in the 19th century.

LEOMINSTER, FROM MILL STREET 1904 51918

The church here is magnificent and dates from the 12th century; it has some wonderful carvings. A fire in 1699 destroyed much of the interior, and led to a decision to demolish the entire building and rebuild the church. Fortunately, the local people were against this plan and raised the £16,000 needed to restore it.

LEOMINSTER, THE PRIORY CHURCH, THE DUCKING STOOL 1904 51934

The ducking stool still survives in the church. It was last used in 1809 for a scolding wife called Jenny Piper. But it was not only used for nagging women. One delightful pub sign in the town depicts a man (a cheating trader perhaps?) undergoing a ducking. Quite right too!

LEOMINSTER, BROAD STREET 1936 87369

Pronounced Lemster, this is the second town in Herefordshire. Many references say the name comes from leo meaning lion, the monastery of the lions. This is wrong, however. Again we go back to that word 'lei' meaning to flow or flood. I have used at least three different spellings for this word - a constant problem with such early, little-known words.

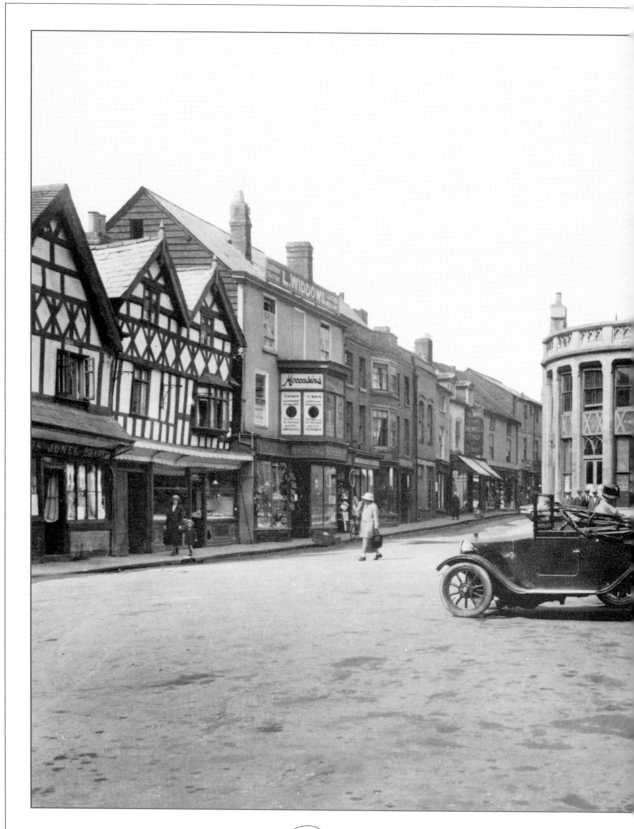

LEOMINSTER, THE CORN SQUARE 1925
76929
This superb building has been replaced by a boring and bland 1960s brick structure - such a pity. It was an old cinema. Is the man sitting in the back of the second car in the photo waiting for his chauffeur, do you think?

LEOMINSTER, VICARAGE STREET 1906 55492
Today, with all our 'mod cons', we never pause to consider the problems of looking clean. Both ladies in this picture have white aprons, even the little girls have clean pinnies on - yet all these will have been washed by hand.

LEOMINSTER 1904 51923

If only those trees had been left alone they would look magnificent now - but they have gone. However, the carved posts on each side of the shop on the right still survive. Notice also the little handcart, parked by the pavement.

LEOMINSTER, OLD HOUSES, CORN SQUARE 1936 87368

I am particularly fond of Leominster - it is one of those towns that should be wandered through at leisure, with regular stops for coffee or tea. It strikes me that every coffee shop in the town sells antiques, and every antique shop sells coffee - a very civilised combination.

LEOMINSTER, HIGH STREET 1904 51920
Bellows & Son on the left would appear
to be a hardware store selling a wide
range of goods. They even have a sign
(just to the right of the shop)
advertising 'free inflating station'. Was
this to pump up the air in bicycle tyres?

LEOMINSTER, DRAPERS LANE 1904 51922
The street name here is a reminder of the importance of the cloth trade to the local economy in times past. A local woollen cloth was of such fine quality that it was known as Lemster ore, and Queen Elizabeth I had her stockings woven from it.

LEOMINSTER, SCHOOL LANE 1936 87374
It seems such a different world today from 1936, when every shop festooned its exterior walls with goods for sale. Here it is a draper's shop. Notice the detail of the carving on the gables of both buildings on the right.

LEOMINSTER, BARGATES 1904 51935
Today this is a very busy road, with all the vehicles being controlled by traffic lights. Notice the cobblestones being used for pavements and guttering.

LEOMINSTER, LOWER BARGATES WEST STREET 1936 87372
This is the same street as the last photograph looking the other way and pictured some thirty years later. The young
trees in the earlier picture have grown quite considerably, and the cobbling has been replaced by proper pavements.

KINGSLAND, THE GATE IN THE TREE c1955 K97012
I never expected to find that this tree would still be surviving nearly fifty years later - but it does. The farm (that can be seen through the open gateway) is very appropriately called Holgate Farm.

KINGSLAND, OLD HOUSES c1955 K97010

In 1955 this would appear to have still been two separate dwellings. Today, it has been transformed into one, and the door on the right has gone. So, too, has the chimney, and some of the windows have been changed. Comparing old photographs with modern views can be great fun.

KINGSLAND, THE VILLAGE c1955 K97017

The farmer is taking his cows home for milking. These are the local breed - Hereford cattle - distinguishable by their white faces and the ridge of white extending along their backs. They have been a recognised breed since the 1700s, descending from a cow called Silver.

KINGSLAND, THE MONUMENT c1955 K97002
The inscription says it all - need I say more! Incidentally, Edward was only nineteen at the time.

MORTIMER'S CROSS, BATTLE OAK 1906 55489

This tree on the battlefield may still survive, but I have been unable to locate it. But it looks very old in the picture so I doubt if it is still there. Notice the neat hedge beside it. Hedge-laying like this has had a recent revival in popularity, and examples are easy to spot all over Herefordshire.

LEINTWARDINE, THE BATHING POOL c1950 L214023

I love this picture of children playing in the pool. I am amused by the fact that the girls are apparently intent on some serious swimming - they are even wearing their bathing caps. The pool is actually all that remains of the River Teme in what was obviously a very dry (and hot) summer.

LEINTWARDINE, HIGH STREET c1950 L214019

Leintwardine sits astride a very ancient route. The High Street is close to the line of an old Roman road, which was once a vital route linking Chester and Caerleon, thus giving the legionary armies easy access into any parts of Wales, north, south or central.

LEINTWARDINE, THE LION HOTEL AND THE BRIDGE c1950 L214018

The Lion has long been popular with fishermen visiting the area. This stretch of the river was once described as 'one of the best stretches of trout and grayling water in the whole country'. Like many rivers, it has suffered in recent years but is now making a comeback; otters are once again being seen along its banks.

CROFT CASTLE, THE EAST FRONT AND ST MICHAEL'S CHURCH c1960 R57505

LITTLE HEREFORD, THE CHURCH 1898 41745

CROFT CASTLE
The East Front and St Michael's Church c1960
The Croft family is mentioned as owning this manor
in the Domesday Book. The family is still there
today, but not without a break. Debts forced them
to sell the house in 1746, and it took them nearly
200 years before they could buy it back. Nowadays
the estate is run by the National Trust.

LITTLE HEREFORD
The Church 1898
Little Hereford is so called because the manor once
belonged to the Church at Hereford, rather than
because it was another army fording place. It sits
beside the River Teme, and the church of St Mary
Magdalene, which was built in the 13th century, has
been regularly flooded over the centuries.

LITTLE HEREFORD
The Church 1898

Here we can just see the church peeping through the trees. The fact that it has survived at all is probably because it serves a relatively isolated and small community that could never afford to rebuild.

LITTLE HEREFORD
The River Teme 1898

A herd of Hereford cattle (notice the white faces) are cooling themselves in the river. This breed was bred both for its meat and for milk. They are particularly hardy animals, and today Hereford cattle are to be found all over the world coping with great extremes of climate.

LITTLE HEREFORD, THE CHURCH 1898 41746

LITTLE HEREFORD, THE RIVER TEME 1898 41747

BREDENBURY COURT C1955 B422001

The name Bredenbury is rather fascinating. Bury (or elsewhere borough or burgh) means a fortified place. Breden, however, is thought to mean that this particular fort was made using boards - in other words, it was probably an old Celtic fort with earthen ramparts that were faced with wooden boards.

BREDENBURY, THE SCHOOL C1955 B422006

The Court is now a private preparatory school. In the early 1900s the house was maintained in lavish style. The household had a butler, housekeeper, valets, nurses, grooms, three footmen and fourteen maids. And I haven't mentioned the gardeners or the people who worked in the stables, the kennels or elsewhere on the estate!

Bromyard to Ledbury and The Malvern Hills

BROMYARD

High Street c1955 B229039
Bromyard was originally the enclosure (yard) where broom
grows. It strikes me as rather an odd way of distinguishing
one place from another when one considers how broom
grows just about everywhere.

BROMYARD, THE SQUARE 1906 54302

Here we see the Hop Pole Hotel - a reminder that Herefordshire was (and still is) an important hop producing region. In 1807 there were 660 acres of hopfields in the parish of Bromyard alone. The young boy standing forlornly outside the hotel has obviously been told to wait while his father has a 'quick' pint.

BROMYARD, BROAD STREET c1906 B229301

Notice how everyone (and there are quite a few people about) is watching the photographer. Even the driver seems to have stopped to pose for the picture.

BROMYARD, BROAD STREET c1955 B229070

This is the same street as in the previous photograph, though looking the other way, some fifty years later; this time, apart from one young boy, everyone totally ignores the camera. The Progress Stores on the right is now the Country Cleaners launderette. Progress indeed!

BROMYARD, SHERFORD STREET 1923 73458

Sherford Street has been considerably shortened since this photograph was taken - the buildings at the bottom of the street were knocked down to make way for a by-pass.

BROMYARD, FROM THE STATION 1906 54301

This line, part of the Worcester and Bromyard Railway Company, was opened in 1877 and was later sold to the Great Western Railway Company. In 1900 there were five passenger trains a day serving this small community, but the line was eventually closed in 1964.

BROMYARD, THE DOWNS 1906 54299

Splendid views of the area can be enjoyed from the Downs, looking both towards the English Midlands and westwards into Wales. Historically it was an area of common land with grazing rights for local people for their animals.

BROMYARD

Jubilee Oaks on the Downs 1923

The Jubilee oaks are now two fine trees. They commemorate Queen Victoria's jubilee some thirty years before this picture was taken.

BROMYARD

The Golf House and the Links 1906

This area has been used for leisure pursuits for around two hundred years now. Early in the 1800s the Downs were used as a racecourse. In 1906 we have a golf course. Today it is a very popular spot for walking.

BROMYARD, JUBILEE OAKS ON THE DOWNS 1923   73452

BROMYARD, THE GOLF HOUSE AND THE LINKS 1906   57116

BROMYARD, SALTMARSHE CASTLE 1923 73468

BROMYARD
Saltmarshe Castle 1923

This lovely building was actually a Victorian gothic fake. It was demolished in 1955, and today only the east and west lodges survive at the entrance to the estate to remind us that it ever existed.

WHITBOURNE
The Church c1955

St John's church is the burial place of an early writer of science fiction. He was a bishop, Francis Godwin, and his book was called 'The Man in the Moon'. In it a man reaches the moon and finds there a paradise where evil people are banished to live on Earth!
Godwin died in 1633.

WHITBOURNE, THE CHURCH c1955 W306011

BOSBURY, THE CHURCH c1960 B420503

A local saying is that you should 'make your will before going to Bosbury'. The church bells ring out 'roast beef and old perry, say the bells of Bosbery'. Perhaps it is too much good living in the village that is the cause of the first quote.

BOSBURY, THE CHURCH, THE LYCHGATE c1960 B420504

A lych was an early word for a corpse. In the past mourners would come to the church and rest the coffin in the lychgate to await the arrival of the priest. He would then lead the mourners to the graveside where the service would be held; early funeral services were seldom held in churches.

COLWALL, THE MALVERN HILLS c1965 C216017
This is one railway line that does still survive. Just after Colwall, the line enters a tunnel, over a mile long, beneath the Malvern Hills. Stephen Ballard, the engineer who built the tunnel, later came to live in the area and fought to protect the hills from over-development.

UPPER COLWALL, THE VILLAGE c1965 C216022

Colwall and Upper Colwall sit beside the Malvern Hills, famous for their Malvern Water. Colwall means cool well or spring; not far from here there is a spring where people can help themselves to the water. The water is supposed to be particularly good for brewing tea.

COLWALL, HEREFORDSHIRE BEACON, THE BRITISH CAMP c1955 C216007

The British Camp is an old Iron Age hill fort, superbly positioned with views in all directions. It is not surprising that it has long been a magnet for walkers from all over the country.

COLWALL, THE BEACON FROM UPPER COLWALL c1965 C216020
The Malvern Hills are especially associated with the composer Edward Elgar. Though born in Worcestershire, he had strong links with Herefordshire too. One of his 'Enigma Variations' (the 11th) is based on the splashing noise of a dog called Dan playing in the river at Hereford - Dan's grave still exists in the city.

EASTNOR, VIEW FROM ABOVE c1955 E107004
A lovely view of both the castle and the church. Although the tower of St John's church dates from the 14th century, the church itself was rebuilt in the 19th century to a design by Sir Gilbert Scott.

EASTNOR, THE CASTLE c1880 12621
A 'princely and imposing pile' is how Eastnor Castle was described when it was built in the early 1800s. It cost £85,923 13s 11½d to build - I love that ½d - and required 4,000 tons of stone, 16,000 tons of mortar and 600 tons of wood. Money was saved by using iron for roof trusses and beams.

EASTNOR
The Gates c1955
Today the castle is still privately owned by the Hervey-Bathurst family; it is opened to the public every summer.

EASTNOR
The Post Office c1955
Isn't it a delightful cottage! The post office is through the door on the left. The sign above the door reads 'Post Office for Money Orders, Savings Bank, Parcel Post, Telegraph, Insurance Annuity and Express Delivery Business'. I think that covers just about everything.

EASTNOR, THE GATES C1955 E107002

EASTNOR, THE POST OFFICE C1955 E107018

LEDBURY, THE HOMEND c1880 L132302

Ledbury has a strong poetic tradition which, according to some, dates from William Langland in the 14th century. It is debatable whether he was connected with the town. But the links with Elizabeth Barrett Browning and John Masefield cannot be denied.

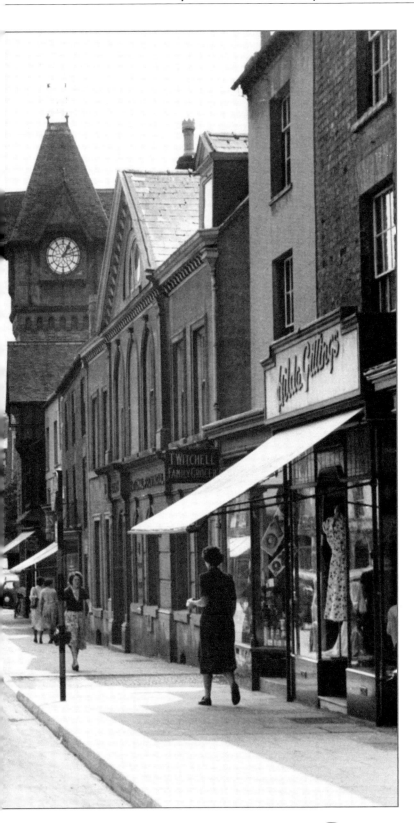

LEDBURY, THE HOMEND 1952 L132027
Elisabeth Barrett came to live in Ledbury as a child; her father called her the 'Poet Laureate of Hope End' (the name of their house). She later eloped with Robert Browning and died in Italy. The clock tower is her memorial. John Masefield was, of course, a genuine Poet Laureate. He was born here in 1878.

LEDBURY, CHURCH LANE 1938 L132004
This street is always appearing in period costume dramas. A painted room was recently discovered in one of the timber houses here - the painting dates from around 1560, and had survived beneath layers of later plastering and wallpaper.

LEDBURY, CHURCH HOUSE c1880 L132309
The churchyard at Ledbury was the scene of a fierce battle during the Civil War when Prince Rupert attacked the Parliamentary forces stationed in the town. The stonework of the church is still pitted with bullet holes, and the church door still has lumps of lead stuck in it.

LEDBURY, THE MARKET HALL 1870 L132002

Compare this Market House with the stone one in Ross. They are both much the same age. This one was built to act mainly as a corn market for the local farmers; income from their rentals was to be used each year to supply twelve local paupers with new coats.

LEDBURY, YE OLDE TALBOT HOTEL c1955 L132020

Ledbury once had two representatives at Parliament. But in 1305 the local people decided against having MPs, saying they could not afford the expense of being represented at Parliament. So much for democracy, such as it was even then!

Index

Frith Book Co Titles

www.frithbook.co.uk

The Frith Book Company publishes over 100 new titles each year. A selection of those currently available are listed below. For latest catalogue please contact Frith Book Co.

Town Books 96pp, 100 photos. County and Themed Books 128pp, 150 photos (unless specified). All titles hardback laminated case and jacket except those indicated pb (paperback)

Around Bakewell	1-85937-113-2	£12.99	English Castles	1-85937-078-0	£14.99
Around Barnstaple	1-85937-084-5	£12.99	Essex	1-85937-082-9	£14.99
Around Bath	1-85937-097-7	£12.99	Around Exeter	1-85937-126-4	£12.99
Around Belfast	1-85937-094-2	£12.99	Exmoor	1-85937-132-9	£14.99
Berkshire (pb)	1-85937-191-4	£9.99	Around Falmouth	1-85937-066-7	£12.99
Around Blackpool	1-85937-049-7	£12.99	Around Great Yarmouth	1-85937-085-3	£12.99
Around Bognor Regis	1-85937-055-1	£12.99	Greater Manchester	1-85937-108-6	£14.99
Around Bournemouth	1-85937-067-5	£12.99	Around Guildford	1-85937-117-5	£12.99
Brighton (pb)	1-85937-192-2	£8.99	Hampshire	1-85937-064-0	£14.99
Around Bristol	1-85937-050-0	£12.99	Around Harrogate	1-85937-112-4	£12.99
British Life A Century Ago	1-85937-103-5	£17.99	Around Horsham	1-85937-127-2	£12.99
Buckinghamshire (pb)	1-85937-200-7	£9.99	Around Ipswich	1-85937-133-7	£12.99
Around Cambridge	1-85937-092-6	£12.99	Ireland (pb)	1-85937-181-7	£9.99
Cambridgeshire	1-85937-086-1	£14.99	Isle of Man	1-85937-065-9	£14.99
Canals and Waterways	1-85937-129-9	£17.99	Isle of Wight	1-85937-114-0	£14.99
Cheshire	1-85937-045-4	£14.99	Kent (pb)	1-85937-189-2	£9.99
Around Chester	1-85937-090-x	£12.99	Around Leicester	1-85937-073-x	£12.99
Around Chesterfield	1-85937-071-3	£12.99	Leicestershire (pb)	1-85937-185-x	£9.99
Around Chichester	1-85937-089-6	£12.99	Around Lincoln	1-85937-111-6	£12.99
Churches of Berkshire	1-85937-170-1	£17.99	Lincolnshire	1-85937-135-3	£14.99
Churches of Dorset	1-85937-172-8	£17.99	Around Liverpool	1-85937-051-9	£12.99
Colchester (pb)	1-85937-188-4	£8.99	London (pb)	1-85937-183-3	£9.99
Cornwall	1-85937-054-3	£14.99	Around Maidstone	1-85937-056-x	£12.99
Cotswolds	1-85937-099-3	£14.99	New Forest	1-85937-128-0	£14.99
Cumbria	1-85937-101-9	£14.99	Around Newark	1-85937-105-1	£12.99
Dartmoor	1-85937-145-0	£14.99	Around Newquay	1-85937-140-x	£12.99
Around Derby	1-85937-046-2	£12.99	North Devon Coast	1-85937-146-9	£14.99
Derbyshire (pb)	1-85937-196-5	£9.99	North Yorkshire	1-85937-048-9	£14.99
Devon	1-85937-052-7	£14.99	Northumberland and Tyne & Wear		
Dorset	1-85937-075-6	£14.99		1-85937-072-1	£14.99
Dorset Coast	1-85937-062-4	£14.99	Norwich (pb)	1-85937-194-9	£8.99
Down the Severn	1-85937-118-3	£14.99	Around Nottingham	1-85937-060-8	£12.99
Down the Thames	1-85937-121-3	£14.99	Nottinghamshire (pb)	1-85937-187-6	£9.99
Around Dublin	1-85937-058-6	£12.99	Around Oxford	1-85937-096-9	£12.99
East Anglia	1-85937-059-4	£14.99	Oxfordshire	1-85937-076-4	£14.99
East Sussex	1-85937-130-2	£14.99	Peak District	1-85937-100-0	£14.99
Around Eastbourne	1-85937-061-6	£12.99	Around Penzance	1-85937-069-1	£12.99
Edinburgh (pb)	1-85937-193-0	£8.99	Around Plymouth	1-85937-119-1	£12.99

Available from your local bookshop or from the publisher

Frith Book Co Titles (continued)

Around Reading	1-85937-087-x	£12.99		Stone Circles & Ancient Monuments		
Redhill to Reigate	1-85937-137-x	£12.99			1-85937-143-4	£17.99
Around St Ives	1-85937-068-3	£12.99		Around Stratford upon Avon		
Around Salisbury	1-85937-091-8	£12.99			1-85937-098-5	£12.99
Around Scarborough	1-85937-104-3	£12.99		Suffolk	1-85937-074-8	£14.99
Scotland (pb)	1-85937-182-5	£9.99		Sussex (pb)	1-85937-184-1	£9.99
Scottish Castles	1-85937-077-2	£14.99		Surrey	1-85937-081-0	£14.99
Around Sevenoaks and Tonbridge				Around Torbay	1-85937-063-2	£12.99
	1-85937-057-8	£12.99		Around Truro	1-85937-147-7	£12.99
Sheffield and S Yorkshire	1-85937-070-5	£14.99		Victorian & Edwardian Kent		
Around Southampton	1-85937-088-8	£12.99			1-85937-149-3	£14.99
Around Southport	1-85937-106-x	£12.99		Victorian & Edwardian Yorkshire		
Around Shrewsbury	1-85937-110-8	£12.99			1-85937-154-x	£14.99
Shropshire	1-85937-083-7	£14.99		Warwickshire (pb)	1-85937-203-1	£9.99
South Devon Coast	1-85937-107-8	£14.99		Welsh Castles	1-85937-120-5	£14.99
South Devon Living Memories				West Midlands	1-85937-109-4	£14.99
	1-85937-168-x	£14.99		West Sussex	1-85937-148-5	£14.99
Staffordshire (96pp)	1-85937-047-0	£12.99		Wiltshire	1-85937-053-5	£14.99
				Around Winchester	1-85937-139-6	£12.99

Frith Book Co titles available Autumn 2000

Croydon Living Memories (pb)				Worcestershire	1-85937-152-3	£14.99	Sep
	1-85937-162-0	£9.99	Aug	Yorkshire Living Memories	1-85937-166-3	£14.99	Sep
Glasgow (pb)	1-85937-190-6	£9.99	Aug				
Hertfordshire (pb)	1-85937-247-3	£9.99	Aug	British Life A Century Ago (pb)			
North London	1-85937-206-6	£14.99	Aug		1-85937-213-9	£9.99	Oct
Victorian & Edwardian Maritime Album				Camberley (pb)	1-85937-222-8	£9.99	Oct
	1-85937-144-2	£17.99	Aug	Cardiff (pb)	1-85937-093-4	£9.99	Oct
Victorian Seaside	1-85937-159-0	£17.99	Aug	Carmarthenshire	1-85937-216-3	£14.99	Oct
				Cornwall (pb)	1-85937-229-5	£9.99	Oct
Cornish Coast	1-85937-163-9	£14.99	Sep	County Maps of Britain	1-85937-156-6	£19.99	Oct
County Durham	1-85937-123-x	£14.99	Sep	English Country Houses	1-85937-161-2	£17.99	Oct
Dorset Living Memories	1-85937-210-4	£14.99	Sep	Humberside	1-85937-215-5	£14.99	Oct
Gloucestershire	1-85937-102-7	£14.99	Sep	Lancashire (pb)	1-85937-197-3	£9.99	Oct
Herefordshire	1-85937-174-4	£14.99	Sep	Manchester (pb)	1-85937-198-1	£9.99	Oct
Kent Living Memories	1-85937-125-6	£14.99	Sep	Middlesex	1-85937-158-2	£14.99	Oct
Leeds (pb)	1-85937-202-3	£9.99	Sep	Norfolk Living Memories	1-85937-217-1	£14.99	Oct
Ludlow (pb)	1-85937-176-0	£9.99	Sep	Preston (pb)	1-85937-212-0	£9.99	Oct
Norfolk (pb)	1-85937-195-7	£9.99	Sep	South Hams	1-85937-220-1	£14.99	Oct
Somerset	1-85937-153-1	£14.99	Sep	Swansea (pb)	1-85937-167-1	£9.99	Oct
Tees Valley & Cleveland	1-85937-211-2	£14.99	Sep	Victorian and Edwardian Sussex			
Thanet (pb)	1-85937-116-7	£9.99	Sep		1-85937-157-4	£14.99	Oct
Tiverton (pb)	1-85937-178-7	£9.99	Sep	West Yorkshire (pb)	1-85937-201-5	£9.99	Oct
Weymouth (pb)	1-85937-209-0	£9.99	Sep				

See Frith books on the internet www.frithbook.co.uk

FRITH PRODUCTS & SERVICES

Francis Frith would doubtless be pleased to know that the pioneering publishing venture he started in 1860 still continues today. A hundred and forty years later, The Francis Frith Collection continues in the same innovative tradition and is now one of the foremost publishers of vintage photographs in the world. Some of the current activities include:

Interior Decoration

Today Frith's photographs can be seen framed and as giant wall murals in thousands of pubs, restaurants, hotels, banks, retail stores and other public buildings throughout the country. In every case they enhance the unique local atmosphere of the places they depict and provide reminders of gentler days in an increasingly busy and frenetic world.

Product Promotions

Frith products are used by many major companies to promote the sales of their own products or to reinforce their own history and heritage. Frith promotions have been used by Hovis bread, Courage beers, Scots Porage Oats, Colman's mustard, Cadbury's foods, Mellow Birds coffee, Dunhill pipe tobacco, Guinness, and Bulmer's Cider.

Genealogy and Family History

As the interest in family history and roots grows world-wide, more and more people are turning to Frith's photographs of Great Britain for images of the towns, villages and streets where their ancestors lived; and, of course, photographs of the churches and chapels where their ancestors were christened, married and buried are an essential part of every genealogy tree and family album.

Frith Products

All Frith photographs are available Framed or just as Mounted Prints and Posters (size 23 x 16 inches). These may be ordered from the address below. From time to time other products - Address Books, Calendars, Table Mats, etc - are available.

The Internet

Already twenty thousand Frith photographs can be viewed and purchased on the internet. By the end of the year 2000 some 60,000 Frith photographs will be available on the internet. The number of sites is constantly expanding, each focussing on different products and services from the Collection.
The main Frith sites are listed below.
www.francisfrith.co.uk
www.frithbook.co.uk

See the complete list of Frith Books at:

www.frithbook.co.uk

This web site is regularly updated with the latest list of publications from the Frith Book Company. If you wish to buy books relating to another part of the country that your local bookshop does not stock, you may purchase on-line.

For further information, trade, or author enquiries please contact us at the address below:
The Francis Frith Collection, Frith's Barn, Teffont, Salisbury, Wiltshire, England SP3 5QP.
Tel: +44 (0)1722 716 376 Fax: +44 (0)1722 716 881 Email: uksales@francisfrith.com

---

See Frith books on the internet www.frithbook.co.uk

TO RECEIVE YOUR FREE MOUNTED PRINT

Mounted Print
Overall size 14 x 11 inches

Cut out this Voucher and return it with your remittance for £1.50 to cover postage and handling, to UK addresses. For overseas addresses please include £4.00 post and handling. Choose any photograph included in this book. Your SEPIA print will be A4 in size, and mounted in a cream mount with burgundy rule lines, overall size 14 x 11 inches.

Order additional Mounted Prints at HALF PRICE (only £7.49 each*)

If there are further pictures you would like to order, possibly as gifts for friends and family, purchase them at half price (no additional postage and handling required).

Have your Mounted Prints framed*

For an additional £14.95 per print you can have your chosen Mounted Print framed in an elegant polished wood and gilt moulding, overall size 16 x 13 inches (no additional postage and handling required).

> *** IMPORTANT!**
> These special prices are only available if ordered using the original voucher on this page (no copies permitted) and at the same time as your free Mounted Print, for delivery to the same address

Frith Collectors' Guild

From time to time we publish a magazine of news and stories about Frith photographs and further special offers of Frith products. If you would like 12 months FREE membership, please return this form.

Send completed forms to:
The Francis Frith Collection, Frith's Barn, Teffont, Salisbury, Wiltshire SP3 5QP

Voucher for FREE and Reduced Price Frith Prints

Picture no.	Page number	Qty	Mounted @ £7.49	Framed + £14.95	Total Cost
		1	**Free of charge***	£	£
			£7.49	£	£
			£7.49	£	£
			£7.49	£	£
			£7.49	£	£
			£7.49	£	£

Please allow 28 days for delivery	*** Post & handling**	**£1.50**
Book Title	**Total Order Cost**	**£**

Please do not photocopy this voucher. Only the original is valid, so please cut it out and return it to us.

I enclose a cheque / postal order for £ . . . .
made payable to 'The Francis Frith Collection'
OR please debit my Mastercard / Visa / Switch / Amex card

Number . . . .

Issue No (Switch only) . . . . .Valid from (Amex/Switch) . . . .

Expires . . . .   Signature . . . .

Name Mr/Mrs/Ms . . . .

Address . . . .

. . . .

. . . .

. . . . Postcode . . . .

Daytime Tel No . . . .   Valid to 31/12/02

The Francis Frith Collectors' Guild

Please enrol me as a member for 12 months free of charge.

Name Mr/Mrs/Ms . . . .

Address . . . .

. . . .

. . . .

. . . . Postcode . . . .

Free Print - see overleaf